The Bird That Spoke Through the Window

Soaring From Within

Dr. Debbie Gooden

ISBN: Softcover   978-1-7960-3343-4
       EBook   978-1-7960-3344-1

Print information available on the last page.

Rev. date: 05/24/2019

To order additional copies of this book, contact:
Xlibris
1-888-795-4274
www.Xlibris.com
Orders@Xlibris.com

Now Suffer That!!

Cancer thought it had me beat, my mind wondered and embraced defeat, but only for a moment did it knock me back, my heart is with God, now Cancer, Suffer That!!!

Cancer, you've had your time with me, the unspeakable pain and strain of my being almost destroyed what I had planned to be, you see, I'm trouble free, God still smiles on me, Now Cancer, Suffer That!!!

Cancer, you were the beast I had never seen before, and repeatedly I would ask, "Why did you come my way?" Well, it has no respect of person, so that detour it would not make, yet, it has given me a reason to write today! It has changed my life forever.

I refuse to park in my pain and live a life of shame. I have Ambition with uncertainty, and confidence comes with this new look, a nice round baldhead, which is now my crown. its okay, I'm blessed and still living anyway, and I can Suffer That!!

Written By
Dr. Debbie Gooden

Its Amazing Love

It's amazing, how you've journeyed back to me. It's amazing, I realize you cannot see, what you really mean to me, you know you hold the key, guaranteed this is not a dream, it's just amazing love.

I remember, your gentle smile, and I remember, we shared time for a while, I held you close to my soul, a young girl full of imaginings and goals, forbidden to love the man of my dreams, its now rekindled it seems. It's real Love, and that's Amazing.

I love you, more than you'll ever know, and I can show you, better than I could before, through all of my trials, and all of my pain, God has given me one more chance to love you again, That's why I can say that its Amazing Love.

Perseverance was the key, and the reason you found me, true love was in your heart, right from the very start, so please understand my heart is in your hand, despite the years in between, our love never did end, an amazing feeling of love all over again.

Written By
Dr. Debbie Gooden

THE DAY AFTER CANCER

The day after Cancer encouraged me to write my thoughts and feelings down, When I'm tired and lonely, and no one is around. The message of truth lies beneath the soul of a man. How do you really know what a person has gone through, if you never seek to understand?

Life can be so cruel at times, and trouble seems to be constantly in the way, but when you know who God is, the focus is no longer on the struggle; it's on the blessing just to see another day.

The day after Cancer was impenetrable and excruciating in so many ways, meanwhile, we keep on running from God's mercy every single day, nonetheless; He said cast ALL your cares on Him helps us to see better days come.

This truth has empowered me to love myself more and more, no matter what comes along, Survival from this fight brought happiness and music to my heart, which will forever be my constant song.

The day after cancer is forever apart of my life, the transformation of my being is continuous, no longer will I return to being the same. God made me influential and resilient though, for I now walk, head held high, lacking no shame, and Cancer? No more….just blessed to be here, the day after cancer came to my door!!

Written By
Dr. Debbie Gooden

LIFE'S SONG

Its easy to be pleasant when life flows by like a song, but the one worthwhile is the one who can smile when everything goes dead wrong.

The test of the heart is trouble, it always comes with the years, but the smile that is worth the praises of earth is the smile that shines through the tears.

Its easy to be prudent when nothing tempts you to stray; from without or within no voice or sin is luring your heart away, but that only a negative virtue until it is tried by pride, for the heart that is worth the praises of earth is the heart that resist desire.

Ella Wheeler Wilcox

THE OLD VIOLIN

It was battered and scared and the old auctioneer thought it hardly worth his while to spend much time with the old violin, but he held it up with a smile.

What would you give for this old violin, and who'll start this bidding for, "a dollar!" "a dollar!", "two dollars!" "two dollars!", now who'll make it three?" Two dollars once, two dollars twice, Going for two? But no, from the room far back, a grey haired man came forward and he picked up the bow, wiping the dust from the old violin, and tightening up all of its strings, he played a melody soft and sweet, as sweet, as the angels sing. The music ceased and the auctioneer, in a voice that was quiet and low said, "Now what would you give for this old violin?" and he held it up with a bow, and someone shouted, "$1000!", and the auctioneer said, "and who'll make it three?" "$3000 once and $3000 twice, going and gone!" said he. The people cheered, but some was amazed, and said, "we don't quite understand?" "what changed its worth?" and the man replied, "It was the touch of the master's hand."

"Now there are many a man which lieth out of tune whose battered and scarred with sin, whose auctioned cheap to a thoughtless crowd much like this old violin. A bowl of pottage, a glass of wine, a game and he travels on, he's going once, and he's goin twice, and he's going and almost gone. Then the master comes and the foolish crowd don't quit understand the worth of a soul and the change that's wrought by the touch of the master's hand."

Myra Brooks Welch

SISTER SISTER

Sisters are like none other on the planet, the love they give comes from the heart, and should never be taken for granite.

Sisters are people that hang in there with you no matter how hard things get. She is that person God puts in your life to love and cherish and never forget.

I love my sister and thank God every day for her. She's beautiful, she's fabulous, and she's my friend, but more importantly, she helped me to live life again!

I don't know what I would do without her lovely spirit, her smile and laughter, together we are like red beans and rice, and it doesn't matter who came before or after.

From one sister to another, no one could ever take her place. You see when God gave me you, it came with possibilities of unimaginable love, when I met you, that's when I knew.

Love you sis!

Written By
Dr. Debbie Gooden

LOVED ME PAST MY PAIN

Life is a mystery; you never know what may come your way. In fact, the encounters you experience help mold you into the person you become, its proof on this day.

My life is nowhere near being perfect, its been filled with many disappointments, it was insane, however; it did not matter to you guys, you loved me past my pain.

I will forever be grateful for your support and love despite disdain, which shows a love that runs deeper than the surface, you've been there through the sunshine and the rain.

I can never repay you for your presence this day, you worked hard for me, sacrificing your money and time; and you know I did not mind.

My goal was to just complete the tasks at hand, realizing its not what you say but what you do that stands.

Although, I did not accomplish everything I intended to gain, you consistently filled my life with peace and joy, kept me laughing past my pain.

Thank you family! I love you guys

Family is not just a group of people related through bloodline, yet; it is individuals that are able to love you past your pain and never count how many times.

Written By
Dr. Debbie Gooden

Cancer a Major Set Back

Cancer a major setback comes with strong intent to kill, despite its determination and poisonous imposition; it will never conquer God's will. When we believe God's way, and our minds are clear, there is no one or nothing that can interfere; my faith and love is unimaginable, for I do not always understand, for cancer loves no one, it seeks to eliminate unlike the touch of the Master's hand.

Cancer will never be my friend; everything about it jeopardizes opportunity, though It gave me appreciation of life enough to increase my knowledge and grow, Enabled me to become a brand new me, better than before.

Cancer made me numb inside, and all I could do was lay down and cry, but why, when Christ died on the cross He did not retreat, He called to His father and gave salvation to me. I was not going to allow this disease to defeat; I am passionate with fortitude knowing, God cannot be beat.

Cancer has no respect of person; and I must be honest, my body trembled with fear, nonetheless; I would not give up knowing God is near. Please understand cancer is serious, and has a fatal impact; so allow God to work His magic because

Cancer Is a Major Set Back!

Written By
Dr. Debbie Gooden

MY FIRST LOVE

As a young girl growing up in the south, I had it all it seemed. The culture back then is what it has always been, and My Dad has continued to be the man of my dreams. I knew when I first looked into his eyes, and to my surprise, my first love had arrived, to guide and protect me, but more importantly, God's creation, he could see.

In my eyes, he could do no wrong, when he is present my world was alright, never saw wrong and was never afraid, you see, he'd never leave me alone I was his prize, and you know that's right.

It was not so much his words that hold true, it was His example, and how He treated my mother the first woman I ever knew. No not one will ever know my first love the way I do, He was that guy, the first to give me what God extends to you, Yep, that's my Dad, through and through.

Measuring up to a man held in high esteem among many, not just another brother, but I'm sure He'd agree, we complete each other. No one could ever take my place in His world, for He is my first love because I will always be his little girl.

Educating his mind was his thing, he was the smart person, relentless to his study, and he knew everything. "Read a book" is what he would say, do not waste time, for time is moving on, I appreciated his dedication and hard work, and despite segregation, he stayed strong.

Dad, he is my kind of man, always looking to fulfill his destiny, and through all his struggles, all I could do was stand by, knowing my day he would soon see, as I walked the stage of life knowing, my dad is proud of me. Many people will never know this man the way I do, He will always be my hero, and what he has given to me, and I can now give back to you. This comes from up above, that is MY Dad, **My First Love!**

Written By
Dr. Debbie Gooden

DECISIONS DETERMINES DESTINY

I have concluded nothing happens by chance, everything you do starts with the idea to advance. What do you do with an idea? Does it grow and multiply over the course of the year? The thought entered the mind to move forward in life, no matter what the price if it seems right, but how dare I move without a plan to guide me, for my decisions determines my destiny!

Tough times don't last, but tough people do, the avenue you choose tells a lot about you. Whether its good, bad, or just plain wrong, You know who you are as you go through the storm, as you grow and change over the course of time, One becomes unrecognizable in their mind. As one transforms from the success the idea brings, as Dad would say, "It was only because your decisions determined your destiny".

Our decisions determines who we become, live life to the fullest and know your freedom has just begun. Who are we if we do not choose our path in life to uphold, we become the person with a story untold. Do you want to be free, if so allow good decisions to determine your destiny.

Written By
Dr. Debbie Gooden

YOU CAN WIN

Cancer came to visit one day, and to my surprise, I could not cry. I guess I was shocked it chose me today and came to my bedside. It knocked me to my knees and I prayed nonstop it seemed; however, I needed to feel free again for cancer is like the world, deadly, evil, and mean.

Cancer is a silent invader that creeps through your body unaware, it simply does not target any certain person; it just does not care. It moves so rapidly and aggressively to destroy, but what should you do. Instantly, respond back, prove that you know how to fight like a girl in this world; never be afraid, and never give in, No matter how hard it gets, You Can Win!

With God, all things are possible. Want He do it, He said He would, over and over again, hold on when Cancer rears its ugly head, no pain, no gain, yet, sustain, live faithfully to the end knowing with Him,

You Can Win!

Written By
Dr. Debbie Gooden

Cancer Is and Cancer Will

Cancer Is:
1. Deadly and painful
2. Determined to Destroy
3. A silent killer
4. Distractive
5. Darkness and changes physical appearances
6. Different and disrupts normality

Cancer Will:
1. Bring families together
2. Increase your faith in God
3. Provide a different perspective
4. Motivates one to live and love life more
5. Make you get on your knees and pray
6. Inspire you to share your story with others

Written By
Dr. Debbie Gooden

ENCANTO SCHOOL THEME SONG

The Reason I Can Fly

Encanto is one of the best school's here, I know its for real, You've helped me to soar! When eagles fly we will spread our wings, where ever we may go, Yeah! Now that I have the confidence to fly, I can now reach for brand new heights, You've encouraged me to take flight!!!

You taught to me to read, you taught me to write, helped to rock the blue, yellow and white, I trusted and believed you'd be right there, because I always knew that you cared. You helped to run, you helped me to rise, helped me to spread my wings up high, because of your love is the reason I can fly.

You'll never know what you've done for me, you believed in me, from beginning to end. And you'll never know the learning I've received, I'll carry it with me, yea, Through the days ahead, I'll always think of you, you gave me hope for something better, There's nothing that I cannot do!!!

You taught me to read, you taught me to write, helped me to rock the blue, yellow, and white, I trusted and believed you'd be right there, because I always knew that you cared. You helped to run, you helped me to rise, helped me to spread my wings up high, because of your love is the reason I can fly.

Written by
Dr. Debbie Gooden

FATHER OF THE YEAR

From a little boy growing up to becoming a man, Having children of his own learning only from his mother how to be the best Dad he can.

If you are one of the lucky ones to have Dad around during these times, you have an example, which helps you be able to live life, motivated, and useful by far, rather than living with resentment and never knowing who you really are.

Growing up must have been difficult for the son who wanted more, and despite his circumstances, giving all he could, appreciating life to the core. But what do you get in return for this loyal and tireless reprimand; nothing my friend, just peace of mind knowing you did all you could as a man.

He vowed to his own children, he would never leave their side. What kind of man is this? One that understands responsibility with nothing to hide. He never split when the going got tough; he just kept going and going despite how rough.

No matter how long it took him, he began to realize a number of things, but he eventually figured it all out; moving gracefully without saying a mumbling word; he educated himself on what manhood was all about.

Hurray! For the man who boldly stands up to the test, although; one of the hardest things to do when there is no one else. This man has a strong belief in God; life being imperfect with no fear, I love him dearly; he is MY…**Father of the Year!**

Written By
Dr. Debbie Gooden

IS CANCER REALLY HERE?

I could not believe it upon receipt. Cancer? I thought it would never come to visit me. It happened so fast that it was almost undetected; but, God sent a little bird to my window with a message, yet, it was not the bird being relentless, instead it was the pain inside that got my attention.

This little bird came to my window at the same time in the morning and at the same time in the evening. At first, I was not sure what to make of it, I was convinced it was seeing its reflection, yet I believe now, it was showing me some affection.

This went on for about three weeks and by the time I was diagnosed, cancer was rising to its peak. The little bird never returned to my window; its mission was complete, cancer had settled in and taken a seat.

The surgeon called the next week to say, "I believe I can help you", but they could only do what they could do. Nonetheless, God works in mysterious ways and this is true. Praying is what I did. When God does something, He does it big, He was in control that day; Cancer had no business attacking me this way.

Cancer was here, but its poisonous venom has gone away. Thank you God for this moment I have to share today, Cancer seeks whom it may devour; and if we allow it, it will stay a while; nevertheless, when you believe in the invisible providence, it discharges from your mind and you keep the power.

Written By
Dr. Debbie Gooden

WE LOOK TO YOU, "DAD"

From the first day we met, honestly, we did not know what we had, but as we grew into maturity observing, experiencing friends, and family trials, we were glad, when no one else was there, We looked to you, "Dad".

Not understanding life at its worst as a lad, wounded and hurt, but we felt protected from the world, we made choices without thinking, losing ourselves in shame, lamenting and mad, but still no worries, in our minds you provided the pad, that is why, we looked to you, "Dad".

Over the years, the times we spent together, through the good and the bad, we listened to your long lectures and speeches that segmented the lashes when you were mad, Oh, how we were mistaken and wrong, to think there was no love. Nonetheless, the message was hidden in the phrase, "Life is like a song without rhythm", that is sometimes ever so sad, that is why, We looked to you, "Dad".

You have given us so much through your example, along with musical talent embedded in our souls, uplifting our spirits, forgive us for our ignorance, for we did not know what we had, for all these things came from you as a lad, that is why, we looked to you, "Dad".

For you have always been the ROCK with a determination, disciplined, desiring, and devoted to bring change, by helping us to use what we carry in us, part of you, like none other in 75 years, aren't you glad? When its all said and done, we share those memories together we had, and no matter what life may bring to us this day, we know, we can always look to you, "Dad".

Written By
Dr. Debbie Gooden

STAND STRONG REGARDLESS OF NEGATIVITY

Life is filled with many hardship and pain, the people we love the most are the catalysts in this disdain, but continuing to love will free our souls best, so forgive and forget and let God do the rest.

Someone told me once that I would never make it, my mind was literally out done with disbelief, the question left to ask was, How could they say that to me?

a person that claim to love me but never supporting my dreams, well we all know what that means. Low self-esteem with a negative attitude, and no plan for themselves it seemed.

Keeping you down and always wondering what could have been, not allowing you to soar and grow from within, but isolating you and your gifts from the world, Stand strong and allow yourself to unfurl.

You see I'm not worried when things go wrong in my life, I just keep praying for those people who bring me strife.

The bible said to pray for my enemies in which I try to do, but sometimes Satan and his evil ways seem to seep thru, by giving permission to others to doubt my ability in everything I do.

Instead of being irritated, it became my motivation to prove everyone wrong, and as I grew older, I realized, all I need to do is stand strong.

Don't hate participate and enjoy the blessings that life has to offer everyone!!!

Written By
Dr. Debbie Gooden

Time to Take a Stand

All my life, I lived trying to please others rather than myself, my feelings were concealed and kept on the shelf. I learned to go along to get along and never allowed myself to stand for the one who loved me the most; everyone else could, except for me, and maybe one day I'll learn the reasons why this came to be.

I moved by the inspiration of acceptance and wanting to be the good girl, and not allowed to follow my heart, and love whom I choose in this world, just told to do this or that. where do I draw the line, when starting to fight back?

From these experiences, I've grown to love them anyway, holding on to this animosity permits stress and sickness to camp out and stay. So, I move on with life giving myself a new start, giving myself permission to share my feelings with whom I want and let true love back into my heart!

Its time to take a stand!!!!!

Written By
Dr. Debbie Gooden

MY STORY

If I could go back in time to live my life all over again, I'd take the time to give God more glory, Life is but a vapor, and I am only here for a short while, I don't have time to waste not giving others a smile.

A smile that inspires, enlightens, and motivates, not one of lies, deceit and hate. I want my life to express a narrative of peace that surpasses all understanding, I never know who's watching, who I am influencing to do the right or wrong things in passing.

Standing for something represents confidence, respect for myself and others, it would be a shame to loose myself on account of another brother,

so I am who I am despite the pressures of this world, and I have been trying to hold on since I was a young girl. Although I have embraced negative influences beyond my control; If you are really listening the real truth is being told, The culture I created was what I allowed, but these things do not embody me, I still stand proud, so through it all, I am still being me, and sure to have done the right things, and that my friend is, heavenly, you see?

I only care about what God thinks of me, its my story He will judge to make me free. Salvation is what I long for in the end, so don't let my life end before you begin. Use my life as an example of what to do in some cases, and what not to do in others, that's how we learn to teach our sisters and brothers.

Written By
Dr. Debbie Gooden

SLAVE MENTALITY

Running free one day and being captive the next, I guess the white man thought, why should we be happy, let's make their lives perplexed. all for money and personal gain the new world was perfect for them, but very painful for us, thanks to strong minded friends, we no longer sit in the back of the bus.

The condition of slavery became racist and mean, so the rest of the world joined this team. Their character was like hitler, if you look like him, well, you were supreme.

Stripped of the right to dream, and forced to think and become less than what I was, I began to fight from within where my power lies and envisage the unthinkable, just because.

Appreciate my nappy hair and my beautiful dark skin, prove to ourselves, not the world, we can win again and again. I was angry and objected being called colored, that's not my name nor is it who I am, why can't we be addressed as a sir or a madam?

Enslaved for years and sold as property, beaten and tormented, forbidden to be human and free has tainted our minds. As a result, we have a thirst for violence, we are inferior to ourselves, our hearts are cynical and unkind.

this life has become unconscientiously the new reality, profoundly, I can say, we have comprised the mindset of a slave mentality!

Unfortunately, children have endorsed killing as the norm over education; on the real, this has become a serious situation.

Severe and thoughtless crimes bringing families to their knees, unbearable loss and casualties.

We cannot continue to allow this history to roll out in the streets and assassinate me, this day we must feel a sense of urgency to change this slave mentality.

Written By
Dr. Debbie Gooden

MYSELF

I have to live with myself and so I want to be fit for myself to know. I want to be able as days go by always to look myself in the eye. I don't want to stand with the setting sun, and hate myself for the things I've done. I want to go out with my head erect, I want to deserve all mens' respect and here, in the struggle for fame and wealth, I want to be able to like myself. I don't want to look at myself and know that I'm a bluster, and bluff, and empty show. I can never hide myself from me I see what others may never see. I know what others may never know, I can never fool myself and so, whatever happens, I want to be self-respecting and conscience free.

Goodie Goodie

Goodie Goodie was her nick name, her presentation of herself was never lame. She always strived to be the good girl, conscience of her actions and how she was received by the world, she just laughed a lot, cursing people out, she would not.

Goodie goodie is what she was, growing up she never did what everyone else did or does. She was the church girl, never drank alcohol, smoked weed, or used any type of drug, even in her older age, she is still as she was.

Goodie goodie!

Sustainment was her position, always wanting to be different, she'd seen a lot in her day, and her example was her petition in her own way.

Her son said she was borderline perfect, everything she did just seemed to be right, never tired of being good, she fought a good fight. Her battles were many one after another, but always took the time to encourage others.

Some say she was ms. Goodie too shoes, but what does that really mean, was she afraid to get down with people and cause a scene. Folks looked at her as a singer who sang her troubles away, one who love church so much she'd stay all day.

Others saw her to be sensitive, sincere, and smart, no matter what happened in her life, she continued to have a forgiving heart. It appeared that individuals took advantage of her at times, but she held her own and towed the line.

Goodie goodie was not a bad thing, it was her claim to fame, and it meant a lot to her to maintain her good name.

Goodie goodie!!

Written by
Dr. Debbie Gooden

Printed in the United States
By Bookmasters